GETTING TO KNOW THE WORLD'S GREATEST ARTISTS

A L E X A N D E R
CALDER

WRITTEN AND ILLUSTRATED BY MIKE VENEZIA

CHILDREN'S PRESS®
A DIVISION OF GROLIER PUBLISHING
NEW YORK   LONDON   HONG KONG   SYDNEY
DANBURY, CONNECTICUT

To Naomi Rebecca, a brand new work of art, with love.

Library of Congress Cataloging-in-Publication Data

Venezia, Mike.
   Alexander Calder / written and illustrated by Mike Venezia.
     p. cm. — (Getting to know the world's greatest artists)
   Includes bibliographical references and index.
   Summary: Examines the life and work of the twentieth-century
artist Alexander Calder, famous for creating the moving sculptures
known as mobiles.
   ISBN 0-516-20966-3 (lib. bdg.)   0-516-26400-1 (pbk.)
   1. Calder, Alexander. 1898-1976—Juvenile literature. 2. Artists—
United States—Biography—Juvenile literature. [1. Calder,
Alexander, 1898-1976. 2. Artists] I. Title. II. Series:
Venezia, Mike. Getting to know the world's greatest artists.
N66537.C33V46 1998
709' .2—dc21
[B]   98-18832
                                           CIP
                                           AC

Visit Children's Press on the Internet at:
http://publishing.grolier.com

Alexander Calder was born in Lawnton, Pennsylvania, in 1898. From the time he was a little boy, he was fascinated by the stars and planets and how machines worked. Alexander Calder invented a brand-new, fun, and exciting art using the things that interested him.

La Bouee Bleue, by Alexander Calder. Painted sheet metal. 240 cm. Christie's Images.
Photograph © SuperStock, Inc.

Alexander, who was always called Sandy
by his friends and family, was best known
for his moving sculptures, called mobiles.
Sandy usually made his mobiles out of abstract
metal shapes and painted them with his
favorite colors.

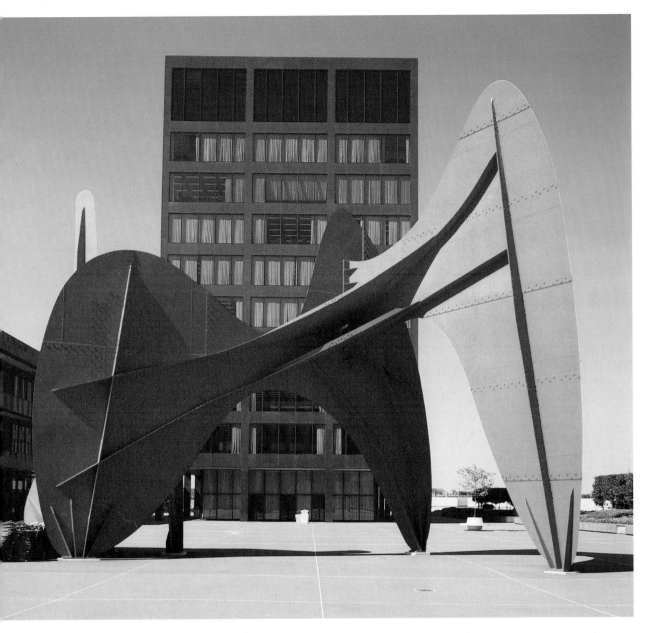

La Grande Vitesse, by Alexander Calder. Photograph by Maynard Williams, © SuperStock, Inc.

Sandy also made sculptures that stood still. These were called stabiles. Some stabiles are as tall as buildings.

Sandy Calder grew up in the perfect family in which to be an artist. Both his father and grandfather were famous sculptors, and his mother was an excellent painter.

Mr. and Mrs. Calder had lots of artist friends, too. Sandy got used to having artists around all the time. At a very early age, he was able to see how paintings and sculptures were created.

The Calder family moved all over the United States while Sandy and his older sister, Peggy, were growing up. They had to be near the cities and towns where Mr. Calder found work creating sculptures. Wherever they moved, Sandy kept busy making toys for himself and Peggy. He found old buttons, cloth, bits of string, and wire, and used them to make all kinds of things.

Toys (installation view), by Alexander Calder. 1904-40. Mixed media. Dimensions variable. University of California, Berkeley Art Museum, gifts of Calder Hayes and Margaret Calder Hayes. Photograph by Benjamin Blackwell.

Sandy and Peggy had lots of pets to play with, too. Once, while they were living in a desert area out West, Sandy made carts out of matchboxes and harnesses out of string. He hooked them up to desert animals he and Peggy found and raced them!

Sandy Calder made clever toys, gadgets, and gifts for people all through his grade-school and teenage years. He decided to study engineering in college, where he learned about designing engines and machines.

After college, Sandy tried all kinds of jobs, but none of them worked out. He ended up moving in with his parents, who were living in New York City at the time.

Bird, by Alexander Calder. c.1965. Photograph © Pedro E. Guerrero.

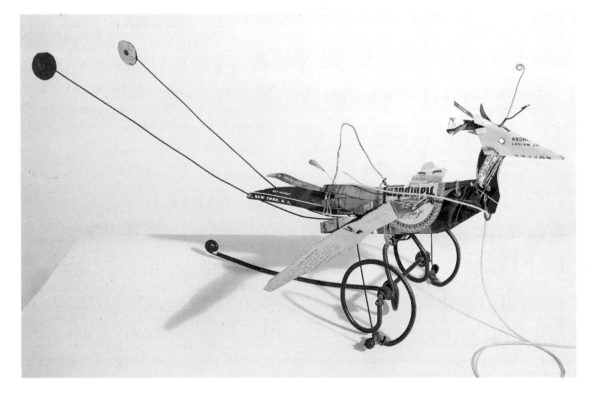

One evening, just for fun, Sandy made a
mask out of paper and yarn, and put it on
the family cat, turning it into a ferocious lion.
Mr. Calder, who was worried about his son's
future, thought Sandy was wasting his time.
He strongly suggested that Sandy start doing
something to improve his mind right away.

To please his father, Sandy decided to take drawing lessons. Soon he discovered he loved to draw! It wasn't long before he became interested in painting, too.

Self Portrait, by Alexander Calder. 1925. Oil on canvas. 20 x 16 in. National Portrait Gallery, Smithsonian Institution. © Art Resource, ARS, NY.

Cutting up Didoes in a City Ice-Skating Rink (detail), by Alexander Calder. New York Public Library, Astor, Lenox and Tilden Foundation.

Sandy Calder went all over New York City drawing and painting city scenes. His favorite subjects were the animals in the Central Park Zoo.

When Sandy Calder was twenty-five years old, he made up his mind to be a full-time artist. He was good enough now to get a job as an illustrator for an important magazine. One of his first assignments was to make drawings of the circus that came to New York. As a kid, Sandy had always liked going to the circus, but now he got a chance to see things up close.

Sandy was fascinated by how the trapeze rigs and safety nets worked. He got to meet clowns and acrobats and saw lions and tigers being trained. The circus inspired many of Sandy's later works of art.

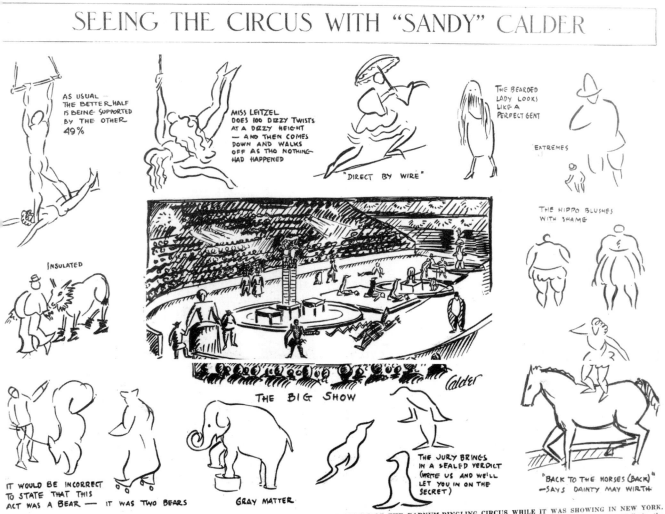

Seeing the Circus with "Sandy" Calder, by Alexander Calder. New York Public Library,
Astor, Lenox and Tilden Foundation.

Lion and Cage from Calder's Circus, by Alexander Calder. 1926-31. Mixed media. Lion: 9 1/2 x 16 1/2 x 5 in. Cage: 17 1/8 x 19 1/2 x 17 1/2 in. Photograph by Geoffrey Clements, © 1998, Whitney Museum of American Art, New York.

Once they knew Sandy was serious about his decision to become an artist, Mr. and Mrs. Calder did everything they could to help their son. They encouraged him and helped raise enough money to send him to Paris, France, which was a great place for artists to be.
In 1926, Sandy left for his first trip to Paris.

At that time, painters, sculptors, actors, musicians, and writers went to Paris to study and see what other artists were doing. Sandy got a small apartment and took a drawing class soon after he arrived. In his spare time, just for fun, he started making circus characters out of wire, cloth, corks, and string.

Calder's Circus, by Alexander Calder. 1926-31. Mixed media. Dimensions variable.
Photograph © 1997, Whitney Museum of American Art, New York.

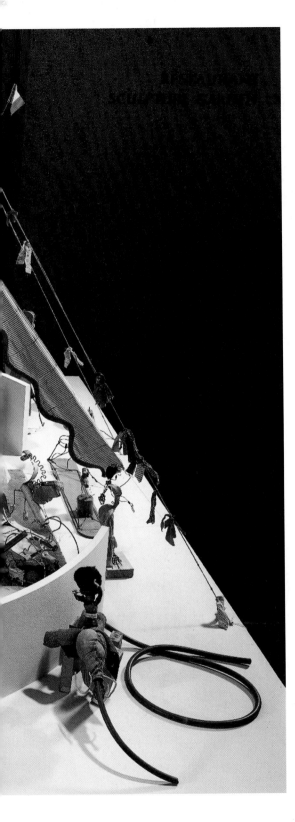

Most of the little circus figures Sandy made could actually do things. Acrobats could swing around and balance on the high wire. Trapeze artists flew through the air and hooked onto their partners. There were clowns, a sword swallower, and a lion tamer, too.

Sandy made everything work with wire, string, cranks, and springs. At first, Sandy put shows on for a few friends. Then more and more people showed up at his apartment. Everyone loved Sandy's sense of humor and the way he made his circus work. It was kind of like watching a three-dimensional cartoon show!

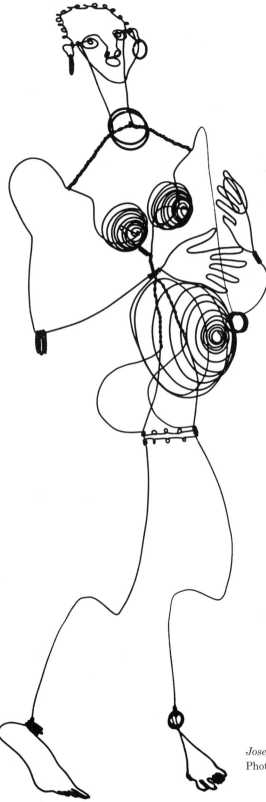

Soon Sandy became interested in making three-dimensional figures out of wire. Sandy liked working with wire. It was something he had been using ever since he was a kid, when he made all those toys for his family and friends.

Josephine Baker, by Alexander Calder. 1926.
Photograph © Pedro E. Guerrero.

Portrait of a Man, by Alexander Calder. 1929-30. Brass-wire construction. 12 7/8 x 8 3/4 x 13 1/2 in. Gift of the artist. Photograph © 1998, The Museum of Modern Art, New York.

Wire Sculpture by Calder, by Alexander Calder. 1928. Wire. 48 1/4 x 25 7/8 x 4 7/8 in. Photo by Geoffrey Clements, © 1996, Whitney Museum of American Art, New York.

Some of the people who came to see Sandy's circus were already becoming famous artists. A few of these artists thought Calder's wire sculptures were great. They introduced Sandy to gallery owners and helped him get his first sculpture show in Paris. The show was a big hit.

Two of the artists who helped Sandy Calder and influenced him a lot were Joan Miró and Piet Mondrian. Sandy liked the colorful blobs and squiggly shapes in Miró's paintings. He loved Mondrian's neat, mechanical lines and pure colors.

One day, while visiting Mondrian's studio, Sandy got a great idea. Mondrian had lots of colored

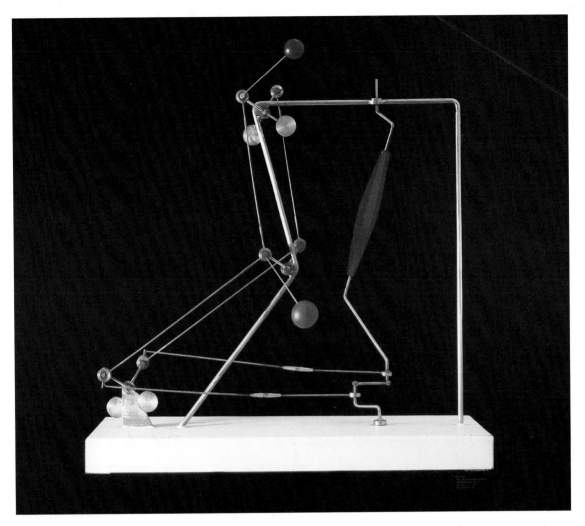

The Bicycle, by Alexander Calder. 1968 (Free reconstruction of "The motorized mobile that Duchamp liked" of c.1932). Motor-driven mobile of wood, metal, cord, and wire. 61 1/2 x 59 x 26 1/8 in. Gift of the artist. © 1998 The Museum of Modern Modern Art, New York.

cardboard rectangles tacked up on his wall. Sandy thought it would be fun if those colored shapes could move around through space somehow. To make his idea come alive, he started making mechanical sculptures that moved with electric motors and cranks.

Sandy's mechanical sculptures were a
big hit, too, especially with his artist friends.
But Sandy wasn't quite satisfied with them.
For one thing, they always repeated the
same action over and over. Sandy thought
his sculptures should be more interesting.

Another problem was that they kept

Lobster Trap and Fish Tail, by Alexander Calder. 1939. Hanging mobile: painted steel wire and sheet aluminum. 8' 6" x 9' 6". Commissioned by the Advisory Committee for the stairwell of the Museum. © 1998 The Museum of Modern Art, New York.

breaking down whenever Sandy had a show. Sandy always brought tools and supplies along to fix them. Soon he had an idea that was really new and different. He decided to make sculptures that floated in space naturally whenever a breeze came along. These were the first mobiles.

Two Moons, by Alexander Calder. 1969. Painted steel. 32 1/2 x 36 x 37 in. ESM. © Art Resource, ARS, NY.

Many of Sandy's mobiles were based on images from the solar system. They fit in perfectly with the times. In the 1930s, everyone was becoming interested in outer space. The planet Pluto had just been discovered. It was the biggest news in years. People were curious to know what else might be discovered in space. They talked about the possibility of space travel and wondered if alien creatures lived on other planets.

Calder's mobiles are amazingly fun to look at. They keep surprising you by dancing around and changing position all the time. You can blow on some of them to help make them move. Some of Calder's mobiles are small enough to hold in your hand, while others weigh thousands of pounds!

Calder mobile in the East Wing of the National Gallery, Washington D.C., by Alexander Calder. Photograph by Ezra Stoller, © Esto Photographics Inc., all rights reserved.

Sandy Calder's stabiles are surprising, too. Even though they're abstract shapes, they often remind people of gigantic insects, birds, or prehistoric animals. It's fun to walk around and under a huge stabile. It kind of makes you feel like you're in a strange world of giant creatures!

Stabile, by Alexander Calder. A & F Pears Ltd., London/SuperStock.

Green Ball, by Alexander Calder. 1971. Aubersson tapestry. 79 x 54 1/2 in., Shirley Polykoff, NY. Photograph © Pedro E. Guerrero.

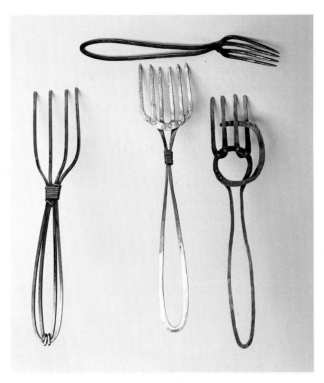

Forks, by Alexander Calder. 1975. Roxbury, CT. Photograph © Pedro E. Guerrero.

Sandy Calder kept busy throughout his life working on all kinds of projects. Besides creating his famous sculptures, he was known for his paintings and drawings, too. He designed wallpaper, rugs, kitchen utensils, jewelry, and sets for plays. He even designed toys that were manufactured by a big toy company.

Plates, by Alexander Calder. 1969. Porcelain. Entrance to Calder's home, Sache, France. Photograph © Pedro E. Guerrero.

31

By the time Alexander "Sandy" Calder died in 1976, he had become one of the most famous artists of the twentieth century. His idea of making fun, colorful shapes move naturally in the air changed the way people thought about sculpture forever.

Calder in his Sache studio, 1976. © Pedro E. Guerrero.

The works of art in this book came from the following museums:

Albright Knox Art Gallery, Buffalo, New York
Museum of Modern Art, New York, New York
National Gallery of Art, Washington, D.C.
National Portrait Gallery, Smithsonian Institution, Washington, D.C.
University of California, Berkeley Art Museum, Berkeley, California
Whitney Museum of American Art, New York, New York